Original title:
Willow Warnings

Copyright © 2025 Creative Arts Management OÜ
All rights reserved.

Author: Charles Whitfield
ISBN HARDBACK: 978-1-80566-777-3
ISBN PAPERBACK: 978-1-80566-797-1

Tales of Tranquil Timbers

In the forest where the branches sway,
A squirrel scolds a bird for being gay.
"Your singing's loud, like a cannon's boom,
It frightens the deer and clears the room!"

Beneath the shade of a gnarled oak tree,
A chipmunk argues over acorn decree.
"I found it first! You can't have a bite!
These snacks are precious, I shall win this fight!"

The raccoons gather, plotting all night long,
To take the prize in the midnight throng.
With masks and capers, they craft a grand scheme,
To steal the snacks and fulfill their dream!

Old badger chuckles from his burrowed cave,
"You silly fools, can't you be more brave?
Take my advice, don't start a ruckus,
Just share your food, or you'll all be trucus!"

Flowers of the Anxious Night

Under the moon, blooms debate,
"Is there life after this date?"
Petals whisper back and forth,
"Let's just take a ride to the North!"

Buzzy bees are late to the show,
Complaining about where to go.
"Why's that flower on his phone?"
"Maybe he's ordering a clone!"

The Lament of the Long Boughs

Branches groan with tales untold,
Hoping for crowns made of gold.
"Why can't we just dazzle and dance?"
"This bark isn't made for romance!"

Swaying to a breeze so soft,
One says, "My leaves are too loft!"
Whispered gossip fills the night air,
As twigs flirt like they haven't a care.

Signs in the Shivering Grove

Rustling leaves plot their escape,
While critters sketch a new shape.
"Is that an owl playing charades?"
"Or a squirrel who's lost his grades?"

Branches waving like crazy arms,
Giggling over their own charms.
A sign reads, "Beware of the gloom!"
"Or perhaps it's just the local raccoon!"

The Portent of the Foliage

Creeping vines are on the prowl,
Daring the sun to throw a scowl.
"Is that a shadow or a friend?"
"Let's toss some leaves for a blend!"

Each leaf a secret, grinning tight,
Hoping to win the grand night fight.
"If you tickle that branch just right,
Maybe we'll dance till the morning light!"

Long Shadows on the Ground

Sneaky shadows creep and crawl,
Lurking low, they play the thrall.
They twist and turn in silly shapes,
Making faces like old grapes.

Watch your step, oh be aware,
Careful now, you're walking where.
Those shadows might just jump and dance,
And pull you in a wacky prance.

A Map of the Heart Beneath

There's a treasure but it's hidden,
A map of love, but it's been ridden.
X marks the spot, but where's the clue?
I swear it said, 'Right under you!'

Hearts are drawn in crayon bright,
Like kids who scribble with delight.
But every note, a little bent,
Keeps leading me on a silly scent.

The Rhythm of the Rustling

Leaves are giggling in a breeze,
Whispering songs that make me freeze.
Each crackle sounds like secret laughs,
Tickling my ears like tiny drafts.

Their dancing moves, a comical sight,
As if they're having a wild fight.
Jumping jigs and silly spins,
Nature's jesters with leaf-like grins.

Sighs of the Skies Marked

Clouds are sighing, who knows why?
 Maybe they've got a pie up high.
 Each puff a muffle, a fuzzy plea,
 'Can someone please rescue me?'

Rain drops stumble, roll, and fall,
 Like clumsy dancers at a ball.
They slip and slide upon the ground,
With splashes, they all dance around.

Lush Layers of Life

In the garden where the branches sway,
There's a dance of shadows in full display.
Beneath those leaves, a chatty bug chews,
Sharing gossip with the friendly dews.

The squawking bird joins in the tomfoolery,
Telling tales of a lost sock, what a foolery!
Bouncing frogs leap with joyous delight,
While flowers wink at the silly sight.

A bumblebee prances, all chubby and round,
Buzzing a tune of hilarious sound.
The squirrel's got jokes, a comedian at heart,
With acorns and puns, he plays his part.

Amidst the giggles of life's grand parade,
Laughter echoes in every glade.
Lush layers whisper of joy and of fun,
Nature's own sketch, where life's never done.

A Sonnet for the Silent

In the stillness where the shadows conspire,
A secret world blooms, sparking desire.
Mice in tuxedos hold a grand debut,
While crickets tap dance, their bow ties askew.

The mushrooms are laughing, yes, quite the trick,
As they plan a tea party with a funny flick.
They giggle and toast with sips of dew drops,
While hanging puffs of smoke from the toadstool tops.

Oh, the grass tickles toes, what a grand affair,
As ants play chess with much pomp and flair.
Life whirls around in a comedy scene,
Where silence has humor, if only you glean.

A sonnet of jest, among shadows and light,
Where the quiet ones rule in their own silly plight.
Listen closely, for laughter hides well,
In the mingled mirth of the woodland's sweet spell.

The Tangle of Tormented Roots

Underneath, a riot of roots and zany tales,
Entwined like childhood friends on playful trails.
They tangle and wrestle, competing for space,
Launching their bids in a madcap race.

The earthworms giggle at the muddled embrace,
While beetles take bets on their frantic chase.
"Who's winning?" they ask through the soil's thin crust,
In this battleground, it's a raucous must.

The roots shout loudly, "Get off my shoelace!"
As they twist and they turn, it's a charming disgrace.
With each crooked inch, they appear to protest,
Yet love is what holds them, it's really the best.

In a tangle of humor, life twists like yarn,
All nature laughs on this ridiculous farm.
So come take a peek at the roots in their fight,
For even the ground has its humorous light.

Beneath the Lush Canopies

Beneath the green, where the squirrels debate,
The wisdom of acorns, oh, isn't it great?
The canopy whispers, tales woven with glee,
Where the shadowy creatures sip sweet chamomile tea.

A chipmunk in glasses reads books of delight,
While a wise old owl nods, his eyes shining bright.
"Life's a jest, enjoy every riddle," he croons,
As snicker of laughter floats up to the moon.

The shadows play games, this hide-and-seek thrill,
While cicadas chirp, working hard for the chill.
Frogs in a band strike up song after song,
In a swirl of antics, where everything's wrong.

So come under cover where laughter runs free,
Beneath these lush canopies, come join the spree.
Nature's a joker with a theatrical flair,
In every green layer, comedy's there.

A Weave of Whispers

Leaves chatter softly, a gentle tease,
Bending with laughter, swaying in the breeze.
A squirrel does somersaults, quite a show,
While the branches giggle, 'Look at him go!'

The shadows play tricks, hide and seek,
As roots tell stories, it's quite unique.
A raccoon in a tuxedo, ready to dance,
Sipping on morning dew, what a prance!

Signs of the Seasons Turning

A robin in shades, struts with some flair,
Complaining of winter, it's just not fair!
The flowers are gossiping, colors in bloom,
While the bugs start a choir, buzzing in tune.

Clouds are plotting, a rain shower prank,
Jumping from puddle to puddle, no rank.
With whispers of spring, it's a party, you see,
Even the old oak winks, 'Join in with me!'

Beneath the Branches' Embrace

A cat in the shade, pretending to nap,
Dreams of catching fish, what a silly chap.
While ants march with purpose, a tiny parade,
Under the canopy, adventures are made.

The wind tells a joke, tickling leaves bright,
As butterflies flutter, taking flight.
A picnic of shadows on grass, what a feast,
With laughter and nonsense, not taking a beast!

Parables of the Pensive Moon

The moon with a grin, peeks through the trees,
Winking at owls who chuckle with ease.
Stars twinkle tales of mischief and jest,
While frogs croak their wisdom, feeling quite blessed.

A firefly's wink, is a wild invitation,
To dance with the night in bright celebration.
As the night starts its giggle, the world spins around,
With a chorus of crickets, making quite sound!

Breaths of the Nightfall

In twilight's glow, the critters jest,
They dance around, no time for rest.
With wiggly worms and crickets' cheer,
Their giggles echo, far and near.

A moonlit stage where fireflies twirl,
Chasing shadows in a playful whirl.
A giggly breeze that tickles the trees,
Nature's laughter rides the night's tease.

Shadows Cast by Time

Tick-tock goes the clock with a grin,
Shadows waltz, it's time to begin.
With every tick, the world's a show,
Where even the stones seem to glow.

Laughter spills where the old jokes lie,
As moments dance like a pie in the sky.
Silly thoughts on this merry ride,
Each tick a twist in time's great slide.

Comfort in the Crooked Ways

Down the path where the funny grass grows,
The plants tell secrets, who really knows?
A squirrel asks me for a potato,
I laugh, then promptly say, "No way, though!"

Twists and turns lead to giggling streams,
Where laughter bubbles, and nobody schemes.
A crooked road, but oh, what a sight,
Full of strange wonders that spark pure delight.

The Enigma of Embracing Change

A caterpillar with a curious dream,
Whispers to flowers, "I might just beam!"
From fuzz to flair, who would have guessed?
That change is the game, and fun is the quest!

A chameleon grins with colors so bright,
Shift and shape as day turns to night.
With every change, a giggle grows loud,
Unraveling mysteries—oh, make me proud!

Beneath the Gnarled Roots

In the shade where secrets play,
Squirrels argue, come what may.
A raccoon capers, full of cheer,
Says, "Don't worry, springs are near!"

Gnarled roots twist like a dancing line,
Each one a hint of the old divine.
A toad croaks loud, it's quite the show,
Proclaiming loudly, "Come see my glow!"

Beneath the branches, giggles coil,
As ants march by in organized toil.
Birds swear they've lost their way back home,
While crickets play their evening poem.

So join the fun beneath this tree,
Where laughter rings so wild and free.
The roots, like friends, all intertwine,
Together here, all will be fine.

A Prelude to Rain

The sky is grumpy, full of frowns,
As puddles wait to sport their crowns.
A hedgehog sighs, "Let's dance in mud!"
While raindrops tease with a playful thud.

Pigeons pouting at the gray,
Socks stuck together, come what may.
Clouds overhead do a little jig,
As thunder rumbles, all loud and big.

Umbrellas sprout like mushrooms in glee,
Swirling colors of red, blue, and pea.
Each child leaps, a splash of joy,
Nature's fancy, with each ploy.

So let it rain, let it pour,
A good excuse to laugh and roar.
Just grab your boots, make a swirl,
A prelude awaits in this big wet whirl!

Whispers of the Weeping Tree

In the breeze, the branches chuckle,
With leafy laughs, a cheeky shuffle.
"Why do you pine?" the tree does ask,
"Just make a joke – that's all I'm tasked!"

Beneath its arms, the critters scamper,
Gathering tales, each one a pamper.
A squirrel shouts, "I stole your acorn!"
The tree just sighs, "Oh go on, adorn!"

Tickling winds relaying whispers sweet,
Tickled toes by the tree's own feet.
With a playful wink, it shakes its leaves,
Saying, "Join us, don't let doubt grieve!"

So come, all ye who long to see,
Life's gentle pranks 'neath the weeping tree.
With every rustle, heed the call,
In laughter's embrace, we find it all!

Shadows Beneath Boughs

The shadows dance in a poley ballet,
While frogs sing loudly, come what may.
Under the boughs, tales come unfurled,
Of sneaky raccoons plotting 'round the world.

A mischievous breeze gives a fragrant tickle,
Promises of giggles, but a quirky pickle.
Squirrels debate in a nutty boardroom,
As branches sway to a silent tune.

In the corner, a snail reads a book,
At the foot of the tree, oh take a look!
With wisdom shared over walnuts cracked,
Every secret and laugh intact.

So swing by the sanctuary, leave worries here,
Let the barky humor be crystal clear.
In the shadows beneath, laughter takes flight,
Where friendships blossom, forever bright.

The Dance of the Silvered Branches

A tree in a breeze, sways left then right,
Its branches like arms, what a silly sight.
Dance on, dear tree, with your leaves all in glee,
I swear they're just laughing, come join the spree!

The trunk seems to wiggle, a shimmy, a shake,
Who knew such a plant could make us awake?
With roots in the soil and limbs in the air,
It's stealing the show, so we stop and stare.

Squirrels join in, they leap with such flair,
Flipping and twisting, they have not a care.
The branches all giggle, the ground starts to sway,
Nature's own party, come join the fray!

So when you're feeling down, just look out the door,
Find a dancing tree and let out a roar.
For laughter grows best in the strangest of places,
Just watch out for squirrels, they're quite full of cases!

Glistening After the Rain

Puddles like mirrors on the ground shine bright,
Reflecting the world in a sparkling light.
A raindrop-topped leaf holds a tiny charm,
A frog leaps right by, with excitement, no harm.

The grass wears a coat, all fresh and so green,
With droplets of joy, like a sparkling sheen.
"Jump in all the puddles!" the children declare,
While splashing about, without worry or care.

But watch for a splash, it might get a bit wild,
Excitement erupts, and you're soaked, oh, what's styled!
"Let's dance in the rain!" now it's thunder, oh dear,
Yet laughter still bubbles, as we shake off the fear.

So after the storm, just go wet your feet,
The world is a playground, a watery treat.
In a rain-soaked delight, let your spirit be free,
For the sun will break through, and there'll be more glee!

Ghosts of the Riverbank

Along the river, where shadows play,
A mushy ghost floats, or so they say.
With a whoosh and a swirl, it glides near the shore,
"Excuse me, kind sir, have you seen my right shoe?"

"Oh phantom, oh specter, I've lost mine too,
They vanished last night, in the dance of the dew.
But let's not be sad, come join the parade,
We'll skip down the bank, in our ghostly charade!"

They glide and they glide, with a flap and a flap,
Waving at fishes, who gaze in a clap.
The reeds sway with laughter; the river joins in,
While the ghosts do their jig with a laugh and a spin.

So if you feel brave, wander out at dusk,
You might spot these spirits, all giddy and husk.
They're not here to scare, just to paint the night bright,
With giggles and splashes, their friendly delight!

Veils of the Twilight Canopy

Under the twilight, the colors all swap,
As the day fades away like a soft, gentle pop.
Stars peek out shyly, giggling in twos,
Dressed up in sparkles, in whimsical hues.

Leaves whisper secrets, oh, what could they say?
"Dance with the fireflies, don't let them stray!"
A flutter, a flicker, they light up the scene,
Swaying and glowing, in a festive routine.

The owls hoot softly, "Let's join the fun,"
With a wink and a nudge, "Oh, we're not done!"
Their feathers all fluff, they too want to play,
In the mocking of night, they dance like ballet.

So wander these woods, let your worries go free,
For humor and magic abound, can't you see?
In the veil of the twilight, let laughter resound,
For the night is a canvas where joy can be found!

The Embrace of the Earth

With roots like shoelaces, tangled and tight,
The ground giggles softly, a mischievous sight.
Each bump and each tumble, a nature's delight,
As squirrels play tag in the radiant light.

Lawn chairs like thrones on this playground of grass,
Where weeds throw a party and flowers all sass.
The worms in the soil share rumors of lass,
While ants create highways, alas, alas!

A tumbleweed's laughter, it rolls just for kicks,
As frolicking critters enact their cool tricks.
The breeze starts to dance, doing wild little flicks,
Nature's a circus, its charm tricks and flicks!

So here in this meadow, where giggles abound,
The chatter of crickets is quite the sweet sound.
The earth wears a smile, its joys unbound,
In this jolly old playground where whimsy is found.

Traces of Trailing Vines

Vines twist and shout like they're joining a band,
A leafy conga line, oh, isn't it grand?
They climb up the fences, in each little strand,
And laugh at the sun, like it's lost in the sand.

With tendrils that tickle the air in their quest,
They prank all the flowers; they're quite the jest.
'We're winning this race', they love to contest,
While bees join the chorus, a buzzing fest!

Each morning, they whisper, "Just watch how we grow,"
As ladybugs bop to the rhythm, you know.
With garden gnomes grinning, all lined up in a row,
It's a wild little party, come join in the show!

These vines have a humor that truly won't quit,
Entangled in laughter, they just want to sit.
A green tapestry woven, and each little bit,
Is a comedy sketch that's made just for wit.

An Invitation to the Inward Journey

The path leads to giggles, where sunlight shines through,
A journey of chuckles, oh, what shall we do?
With breadcrumbs of laughter to guide us anew,
We'll skip like old frogs on a leaf-covered shoe.

Each step is a tickle, a moment divine,
With maps made of folly, each glance, oh-so-fine.
Through puddles of giggles, we'll weave and align,
In search of the treasures where fancies combine.

The forest sings snippets of song through the trees,
And squirrels are holding their own little tease.
With shadows that dance, making fun of the breeze,
This invitation sways us with playful decrees!

So come all ye wanderers, let's ramble and roam,
Together we'll frolic and craft a new home.
In this land full of giggles, no need to feel gloam,
For laughter's our compass; we'll never feel alone.

Beneath the Arching Canopies

Beneath leafy umbrellas, the laughter's a joke,
Where sunlight's a giggle, and shadows invoke.
The branches are chuckling, the wind a soft poke,
It's a comedy club, where all trees partake, folks!

In the audience, critters, with popcorn, they cheer,
As branches tell tales that are silly, oh dear!
The rustle of leaves is the sound we all hear,
A punchline with each gust, it's fun that's sincere.

The squirrels stand up for their stand-up routine,
And mushrooms play piano, it's quite the scene!
With laughter so hearty, it's fit for a queen,
Under canopies arching, where humor's so keen.

So join in the revelry beneath nature's frown,
Where smiles are the currency and jesters don crowns.
It's a place of hilarity just wearing it down,
A canopy kingdom, where giggles abound!

The Telltale of Twigs

In a garden full of chatter,
Twigs tell tales of silly things,
Whispers of a hidden patter,
As squirrels plot their woodland flings.

One little twig just couldn't wait,
To jump into a playful fray,
But got stuck sharing a plate,
With a confused old cat named Ray.

The ants had their own grand parade,
Marching past with tiny flair,
While the tree was quite dismayed,
At all the ruckus in the air.

In the chaos, laughter grew,
As the sun began to shine,
With twigs that waved and flew,
To join the fun, just fine!

Echoes of Soft Sighs

Beneath the branches, laughter flows,
Soft sighs blend with rustling leaves,
  A chatterbox of breezy prose,
   Busy trees wear funny sleeves.

 A squirrel squawked a jest or two,
   Daring all its friends to play,
  While the birdies sang anew,
    In their own peculiar way.

A breeze tickled the bark so sweet,
And made the shadows dance about,
  Nature's irony, quite the treat,
 As giggles turned to joyful shout!

   In this playful, leafy choir,
  Where echoes of dreams collide,
  The soft sighs pulled us higher,
    On wings of joy, we glide!

Secrets in the Green Canopy

In the green above, secrets swirl,
Where giggles hide and whispers bloom,
A chubby raccoon starts to twirl,
Under sun's warm and cozy loom.

Leaves dance like hats upon their heads,
As critters plan a playful quest,
They trade their snacks for tiny threads,
While time slows down to take a rest.

A rabbit hops with comic flair,
Chasing clouds that drift so slow,
He stumbles, then sits with a stare,
At a butterfly's vibrant show.

The canopy whispers and grins wide,
With secrets of laughter and cheer,
While dappled light plays our guide,
In this haven of jest and dear.

The Dance of the Dappled Light

Amidst the trees, a jig takes flight,
As dappled light begins to play,
Frogs in the pond leap left and right,
While shadows join in on the sway.

Fireflies twinkle like little stars,
As a raccoon leads the parade,
All the critters wear their scars,
From wacky games in sunlight laid.

The elder tree tells witty tales,
Of squirrels who forgot their nuts,
As laughter punctuates the gales,
And everyone's stuck in a rut!

So come, dear friend, dance with delight,
Underneath this leafy dome,
Where the world spins in sheer, silly light,
And nature calls us all to roam!

The Stories That Branch

In the garden, gossip flows,
Branches whisper, and it shows.
Leaves share secrets with the breeze,
Tickling toes of buzzing bees.

Squirrels plot their acorn games,
Chasing shadows, calling names.
With each rustle, laughter's found,
Nature's jokes, without a sound.

Old knots from ancient days,
Tell tall tales in winding ways.
If trees could chuckle, oh what fun,
They'd share their tales 'til day is done.

Sunset's glow ignites their mirth,
Chirping crickets break the earth.
Underneath the dancing stars,
A chorus of the tree's memoirs.

Cradles of Unseen Moonlight

In shadows soft, the night does creep,
The moon chuckles, secrets keep.
Laughter winks from leafy beds,
Crickets' hums dance in our heads.

Beneath those branches, dreams take flight,
Bamboozled by the silver light.
Owls exchange their witty puns,
While dreaming of their midnight runs.

A breeze spins tales of what's to come,
With every twist, a giggle's drum.
The stars above wink in delight,
At our shenanigans in the night.

So let's sway under this sky,
Where ancient whispers make us sigh.
In the cradle of the moon's embrace,
Find joy in this silly, playful space.

Echos from the Bark

Old tree trunks have stories bright,
Each scratch and crease holds pure delight.
In bark, there's laughter, wisdom shared,
Of pranks and games that nature dared.

With every creak, a joke appears,
Splintered laughter through the years.
Squirrels snicker at the clumsy cat,
Nature's humor, imagine that!

As woodpeckers tap with glee,
The rhythm echoes endlessly.
Beneath the shade, we laugh and tease,
Bonded by old, swaying trees.

So gather round the trunk so grand,
Where echoes of laughter always stand.
With silly tales beneath the sky,
Life's lightness soars, reaching high.

Signals of the Swaying Bow

The branches dance, a wiggly show,
Sending signals from below.
Watch out for the falling leaves,
They're plotting pranks, let's not believe!

Boughs bend low to share their schemes,
Suggesting fun, with giggles and dreams.
But careful now, don't take a snooze,
You might wake up in a leaf-filled ruse!

Cracks and creaks are laughter's song,
Nature's jesters all night long.
With every sway, a sly little quip,
Swaying bows join in our trip.

So tip your hat to each swaying limb,
Join their laughter, don't be grim!
For in these trees, our joy takes flight,
With branches tickling the face of night.

Threads of Thyme and Time

In a garden where laughter grows,
A thyme that tickles when the wind blows.
Each sprout a joke, each leaf a pun,
Sunshine smiles, oh what fun!

With a twist and a twirl, they sway,
Making faces at clouds all day.
The bees wear hats, the bugs dance too,
In this patch, even rabbits woo!

Tangled yarns create a spree,
Knitting giggles, endlessly.
Time's thread unravels with each jest,
In this garden, we're truly blessed.

So if you wander through this space,
Look for humor in each place.
For laughter's woven in every vine,
Threads of thyme and giggles intertwine.

Between the Knotted Twists

In the woods where branches play,
Knots abound in a merry array.
Each twist a tale, mildly absurd,
Rumors fly on the wind like a bird.

Squirrels chatter with knotty intent,
Plotting mischief wherever they went.
Tangled tales and tangled trees,
Who knew nature could tease with ease?

Between the twists, a joke takes flight,
As shadows dance in fading light.
A raccoon chuckles at the fuss,
While frogs croak out their big plus.

So come and join this lumbering crew,
With knotted paths and laughter too.
For every turn leads to a jest,
In this woodland, we're truly blessed.

Lessons from the Lichen

On the bark where lichen grows,
Wisdom seen in fuzzy prose.
Little jokes on every tree,
Nature's jesters, wild and free.

In shades of green and gray they thrive,
Making sure the humor's alive.
A patchy coat, so cozy and bright,
Who knew wisdom could feel so light?

They softly chuckle without a sound,
Teaching patience all around.
With footsteps slow, we learn to see,
That laughter's roots grow naturally.

So let's take heed from these vibrant gems,
In our lives, where laughter stems.
For in the lichen's quirky cheer,
We find the fun that's always near.

The Softness of Dusk's Cloak

As the day wraps in its cloak,
The sun takes a bow with a gentle poke.
Stars giggle as they blink awake,
Ready to tease, for night's sweet sake.

Shadows grow long, stretching wide,
Even the moon can't help but glide.
Whispers and chuckles fill the air,
As night creatures dance without a care.

Dusk softly settles with a grin,
Chasing away all the day's din.
Fireflies wink, playing hide and seek,
In this twilight, laughter's unique.

So let's bask in the dark's delight,
With silly tales that take their flight.
For in the dusk's warm, snug embrace,
We find the humor in every place.

Beneath the Weeping Branches

Under branches that seem to pout,
Squirrels chatter, they scream and shout.
A raccoon with a hat made from twine,
Claims he's the king, oh, how divine!

The branches shake, they twist and sway,
As birds gossip about their day.
A worm in the dirt takes a peek,
Saying, "I'm just too tired to speak!"

Rabbits gather for a quick debate,
About which veggie tastes first-rate.
They argue fiercely, then take a break,
And split a carrot—oh, for goodness' sake!

Beneath the shade, the laughter flows,
Nature's jesters strike some silly poses.
While the leaves giggle in the light,
It's a circus under the tree, what a sight!

Shadows of the Old Tree

In the shadow of the ancient oak,
A sly old fox shares a joke he spoke.
He says, "Why did the chicken cross the road?"
"To get to the other side, of course, it's code!"

The breeze laughs softly, whispers in glee,
As butterflies dance from branch to tree.
A chipmunk rolls on his back with delight,
While all the critters join in the night.

Rabbits painting with mud, oh my!
A masterpiece, as clouds drift by.
Each stroke is absurd, crooked, yet bold,
A canvas of antics, a sight to behold!

The old tree chuckles, its branches shake,
In this circus, there's no mistake.
Life is a comedy under the shade,
Where laughter and joy are splendidly made!

Whispers in the Breeze

The breeze tickles the ends of my nose,
As the leaves debate about who knows woes.
A ladybug claims she's seen it all,
While a grumpy caterpillar refuses to crawl.

In whispers of laughter, secrets unwind,
A tale of a snail who twirled and declined.
"Oh, I tripped over my own silly shell!"
And everyone cheered, "That was swell!"

The toad croaks, "What's up with the sky?
Looks like nature is now asking why!"
Caught in the humor of life's great tease,
Nature's comedy plays with ease.

As critters share stories, the light starts to fade,
Beneath the canopy, laughter's made.
With giggles and chuckles, they stir up a cheer,
Beneath swaying branches, where all is clear!

Messages Carried by Leaves

Leaves flutter down with a giggly shell,
Carrying whispers—secrets to tell.
A grasshopper leaps with a puzzled frown,
"What on earth, did the foliage drown?"

A beetle wheels in, bright as can be,
"I'm the messenger, can't you see?"
He's dressed in armor, shiny and fine,
Delivering laughs, a winged ale-swine.

A breeze drifts by, it's telling a tale,
Of turtles in tutus, swimming the gale.
They waddle in style, making quite the splash,
While the river giggles, doing its splash.

Underneath this leafy confab of cheer,
All creatures unite with a raucous jeer.
They swing through the branches, dance with the sun,
In this garden of jest, they all have their fun!

Fractured Reflections

In the mirror of a pond, I spy,
A fish with eyebrows raised up high.
It seems to judge my every move,
As I attempt my best dance groove.

A frog croaks out a cheeky tune,
While dragonflies spin like a cartoon.
The turtles point and giggle too,
What am I, a circus to woo?

My splashes echo, a ruckus here,
Critters laugh at my clumsy steer.
I throw in some twirls, and a slip,
The dance party shifts, I lose my grip.

But with each flop and every flop,
Nature giggles and won't stop.
Who knew reflections could be so spry?
Next time I'll just wave, not fly!

Sentinel of the Stream

A stick stands tall, with eyes so wide,
Guarding a stream like a foolish guide.
It wobbles when the water swells,
And whispers secrets the current tells.

A squirrel scurries, it takes its place,
Casting side glances at the stick face.
"You think you're tough? Just look at me!"
The stick just quivers, gleefully.

A beaver floats past with a grin,
Chomping wood, saying, "Where've you been?"
The stick just chuckles, it won't budge,
"I'm more than a log, I'm a rare judge!"

Yet every day, it's a slightly new test,
With fish doing flips, it's never a rest.
Through wave and ripple, it stands so remarkable,
Who knew a stick could be so unshakeable?

Beneath the Lamenting Tree

Under a tree with a great big frown,
Lies a seat made of roots, slowly wearing down.
I take a rest, but it creaks and moans,
As if it's sharing all its groans.

A squirrel passes, with snacks in tow,
"Get off my seat, that's my cozy show!"
I laugh at the branches, twirling in air,
They swish and sway, full of despair.

The tree sighs deeply, dropping a leaf,
"Oh, humans again, we're in disbelief!"
I tell it a joke to lighten the mood,
But it just rustles, feeling quite rude.

Yet every so often, it squeaks out a grin,
I think it enjoys this quirky spin.
So beneath the tree, I'll share some more,
With a friend like this, who needs folklore?

A Tinge of Foreboding

The clouds roll in with a cheeky grin,
Tickling the leaves, suggesting a spin.
The wind starts giggling, full of dread,
"Brace yourself, sunshine, I'm taking your bed!"

Raindrops fall like playful foes,
They splash and dance, while nature glows.
A thunderclap yells, "Time to retreat!"
But the flowers laugh, on their tiny feet.

As puddles form, creatures engage,
Splishing and splashing, they're ready to rage.
A worm slides by, with a wink of glee,
"Get soaked with me, oh, carefree!"

So even with storms that holler and shout,
There's humor found when we twist about.
For nature paints dramas with each drop and beam,
And in this chaos, we swim in a dream.

The Lullaby of the Swaying Grass

In the field where grass does dance,
A bumblebee took a chance.
He landed on a dandelion,
And it puffed out like a lion.

The grass sings in whispers soft,
While cows munch and look aloft.
A chicken joins in with a cluck,
As the wind gives them all a tuck.

The ants parade in a line so neat,
While crickets play their upbeat beat.
A goat can't help but pirouette,
As the sun begins to set.

With laughter echoing 'round the glade,
Nature's jokers all invade.
The grass sways low, the skies turn pink,
Join the fun, come out and wink!

When the Sky Grieves

The clouds wear frowns, oh what a sight,
As raindrops drip with all their might.
A sunbeam pokes its cheeky head,
And steals a kiss before it fled.

Puddles form like giant eyes,
Reflecting all the sullen skies.
A squirrel jumps with a splash so grand,
While umbrellas dance, a crazy band.

The thunder claps, it starts to roar,
A gray mood trying to explore.
Yet blushing flowers peek and tease,
"No worries here, just feel the breeze!"

When skies are sad, they lose their game,
Yet nature laughs, and that's no shame.
So bring your joy, don't wear the gloom,
Let's make some sunshine in this room!

Tides of Emotion

The ocean waves are in a fuss,
As seagulls squawk and make a fuss.
A starfish donned a fancy hat,
Said to the crab, "How about that?"

The tide pulls back, it plays a trick,
While dolphins leap, they're feeling slick.
A jellyfish with flair does glide,
A fish flips by, all full of pride.

Salty tears from the ocean floor,
Lamenting waves crash more and more.
But then a whale starts to dance,
And all the sea joins in the prance.

With every wave, emotions swell,
A quirky sight, we know so well.
So ride the tide, embrace the play,
For every wave brings a new day!

The Weight of Forgotten Dreams

In a corner, dreams piled high,
Some have wings, and some can fly.
A unicorn's wearing silly shoes,
Whispering secrets to a pair of blues.

A cat naps on a sleeping hope,
While fish have formed a daring rope.
Each thought a balloon, too much to bear,
Floating around without a care.

Stacking wishes like a tower high,
A doughnut comet zooms on by.
If dreams feel heavy, take a peek,
They bounce like jelly, not so bleak.

So gather 'round your lost desires,
Light them up like twinkling fires.
For every faded laugh and scheme,
Holds a giggle hidden in a dream!

Unraveled by the Gentle Wind

A twirl of leaves, a gusty tease,
They dance around like squirrels in leaves.
With whirls and swirls, they float and dive,
Chasing dreams like a playful hive.

Oops! There goes my hat with glee,
Caught in the branches of a giggly tree.
It giggles back like a friendly ghost,
As I chase it down, at least I'm not toast!

A breeze tickles my nose, oh what fun,
A tickle fight with the day's soft sun!
The branches sigh with laughter, glee,
As I trip on roots like they're after me!

But with each laugh, the world seems bright,
Thanks to a wind that chalks up delight.
In nature's game, I've lost my pride,
Yet every stumble is worth the ride!

Guardians of the Wistful Light

There's a squad of trees, oh what a sight,
Waving their arms to the left and right.
They guard the beams of dodgy sun,
With shadows that stretch and weave for fun.

They gossip with birds, who never seem shy,
While squirrels eavesdrop with a twitching eye.
"Watch out! It's going to be a hot day!"
They holler at clouds, "Come out and play!"

In the midst of their chatter, a new plan thrives,
To fill the air with tickles and jives.
With rustling laughter, they clutch at the light,
Turning shadows into a silly dance fight!

And when the sun dips low, serving drinks of gold,
They rattle their leaves, "Stay curious, be bold!"
These guardians of glee cast spells at dusk,
Turning worries into whims with natural trust!

Fronds that Touch the Sky

Fronds wave high, like kites in a race,
Reaching for heavens, a leafy embrace.
With each gentle flick, they tease the blue,
Making clouds giggle like they always do.

"I'm taller!" shouts one, twisting in pride,
While another fluffs up, "Look, I can glide!"
In the tussle of heights, they swing and sway,
Turning the air into a playful ballet.

They whisper secrets to passing bees,
Who hum back sweetly, "Oh, if you please!"
With pollen and sunbeams, they share a grin,
As breezes blow softly, letting the fun in.

Laughing with dusk, they begin to unwind,
Our leafy comedians, so playful and kind.
When night descends, they'll cradle soft sighs,
These fronds are the jesters who tickle the skies.

Lush Echoes of Longing

In the twilight shadows, a hush comes alive,
With whispers of laughter, in every dive.
The rustling leaves murmur tales of delight,
Echoing dreams in the softening light.

"Oh, remember the time we danced in the rain?"
Quips one leaf to another, like a soft refrain.
With dewdrops as diamonds, they twinkle with glee,
Recalling their adventures, as wild as can be.

"Let's plan a parade when the moon's on the rise,
With fireflies twinkling like stars in disguise!"
They giggle and sway, plotting their spree,
In the echo of longing, wild spirits run free.

And as day departs, their hopes intertwine,
Creating a magic, frothy as fine wine.
These lush echoes linger, that's easy to see,
In nature's green theatre, where we all dance with glee!

Gentle Shadows at Dusk

Leaves dance freely, oh what a sight,
Sneaky critters hiding left and right.
The sun dips low, an amber glow,
Whispers float softly, just like a show.

Silly squirrels chase their tails in glee,
While owls hoot loudly, 'Can you hear me?'
A frog wears glasses, thinks he's quite sage,
Nature's own humor, a comical stage.

Nature's Silent Alarms

Buzzing bees won't stop to relax,
They're plotting mischief, don't cut them slack.
Crickets play tunes, oh how they croon,
While mice use the moonlight as a cartoon.

A fox on a skateboard, what a bold feat,
Chasing his dreams, oh isn't he sweet?
Rabbits hold meetings under the stars,
Laughs echo softly, like musical bars.

Beneath the Shimmering Veil

Fireflies twinkle like little stars,
They gossip and giggle, 'Did you see Mars?'
A slow-moving snail breaks into a dance,
While flowers laugh softly at chance romance.

Frogs wear their tuxedos, looking so fine,
Ready for parties, oh how they shine!
Butterflies flit, their colors so bright,
Staging a fashion show, pure delight.

The Language of the Wind

Swaying branches sharing their tales,
Making up stories that never fail.
The wind whispers secrets, oh so sly,
Curls through the trees, like a playful spy.

Clouds wearing top hats float on above,
While raindrops giggle, share their own love.
A breeze does the cha-cha, just for fun,
Nature's own party, everyone's won!

Memories in the Mist

In the fog, all secrets waltz,
Lettuce hats for garden gnomes.
Whispers float like dancing saucers,
Mice in shoes play house and homes.

Ghosts of noon sip lemonade,
Chasing shadows in a cartwheel.
Socks and sandals on parade,
Laughter bounces with a squeal.

Clouds take turns to dress in style,
Breezes painting grins on trees.
Funny hats make murmurs smile,
Swaying leaves nodding with ease.

Stillness hides a giggling stream,
Jellybeans stumble on their dreams.
In the haze, all's not as it seems,
Moonlit mischief always gleams.

The Gaze of Gnarled Limbs

Branches stretch, they scratch their chins,
Muttering tales of silly wins.
Crows in coats of plaid take bets,
On how long the squirrel forgets.

Tangled roots plot a new play,
With acorns rolling light and gay.
Each twist and turn a punchline waits,
Nature's jest, it celebrates.

While bark-covered spies make their calls,
A squirrel naps, he'll miss it all.
Caterpillars throw a feast,
On leaves as guests, they munch and feast.

The sun peeks through a leafy grin,
Tickling moss where snails begin.
Through voices soft as an old lute,
The laughter blooms, just run and scoot.

Lurking Beneath the Calm

Ripples giggle, fish make waves,
Bubbles burp and water braves.
Turtles tie their hats and scoff,
As a frog declares a dance-off.

Silence shivers with a jig,
While minnows wiggle in a gig.
Frogs in choir sing a tune,
To startle crickets by the moon.

A dragonfly in polka dots,
Swoops and swirls, tying knots.
Under lilies, secrets play,
Beneath the calm, the jesters sway.

Even the pond's got jokes to share,
In hidden depths, excitement's rare.
So next time you sit and stare,
Remember laughter's always there.

Surrender to the Stillness

In quiet moments, jokes unfold,
With stillness round, stories retold.
An ant in shades walks, so chic,
While beetles gossip, oh so sneaky.

Sunbeams stretch across the glade,
Tickling grass as shadows fade.
A stoic rock holds court with pride,
As breezes whisper here and hide.

Frogs exchange their best punchlines,
While crickets keep their rhythm fine.
A deal struck under the shade,
For laughter that won't ever fade.

Embrace this calm, a giggle sprout,
In silence, let your joy break out.
For in the stillness lies the key,
To find a funny side that's free.

Beneath the Swaying Veil

Beneath the branches, a dance so small,
Leaves whisper secrets, a giggle, a call.
A squirrel in a hat, quite proud and absurd,
Mocks the shy breeze with the oddest of words.

Tiny bugs strut on a petal parade,
Winking and nodding, they're not even afraid.
While ants form a line, all serious and straight,
Yet one slips and falls, oh, what a fate!

Dappled light sparkles, a stage set for fun,
With shadows that play, and the day's just begun.
A grumpy old toad sits, stuck in a clutch,
Croaks a complaint, but it doesn't get much.

So if you wander beneath this lush veil,
Join in the laughter, let joyous hearts sail.
For nature's a jester, a trickster of cheer,
With antics so grand, they'll tickle your ear.

The Solitary Sigh of Autumn

Autumn arrives with a tumble and roll,
Each leaf takes a bow, in its fiery stroll.
A pumpkin decides it's a prince in disguise,
Flexing its roundness, oh what a surprise!

Squirrels with acorns are hoarding their snacks,
Planning for winter, they're plotting attacks.
One trips on its stash—a half-hearted flop,
As friends laugh aloud, 'Best leave that on top!'

Ghosts in the garden, all cloaked in their sheets,
Scaring the crows and the stray little fleets.
A scarecrow's missing his head for the show,
But he still strikes a pose—what a star of the row!

So raise up your mugs filled with cider so sweet,
Toast to the leaves that dance at our feet.
For laughter's the spice in this brief autumn tale,
With nature's oddities, we'll giggle and grail.

Nature's Gentle Reminders

The trees nod and wink, in a whimsical jest,
While flowers compete for the title of best.
A bee in a bowtie, quite dapper and spry,
Buzzes around like it owns the blue sky.

The breeze carries gossip from flower to tree,
Of squirrels who strut with a grand sense of glee.
They think they're the stars of a woodland ballet,
But trip on their tails, oh, what can we say?

Clouds wear their hats, all fluffy and bright,
Casting odd shadows that dance with delight.
While crickets compose a most curious tune,
That makes frogs tap dance beneath the warm moon.

So take in the laughter that nature provides,
In moments like these, joy effortlessly strides.
You'll find gentle nudges in silence and sound,
Where the funny and trivial beautifully abound.

The Pulse of the Canopy

The trees hold a rhythm, they sway and they sway,
With branches that shimmy in beautiful play.
A sloth in the crowd, oh, what a spectacle!
Moves like a cloud, though quite unrespectable!

Chirping and tweeting, the band starts the show,
While ants in tuxedos march neatly in row.
The sun plays a tune with its golden bright rays,
Tickling the leaves in a wild, dizzying haze.

A raccoon in glasses debates with a cat,
On who's the best at stealing a hat.
The laughter erupts, and all creatures align,
For a party in branches so splendidly fine.

So sway with the trees and let spirits be free,
Join in the fun, dance along with the glee.
For life in the canopy thrives in delight,
With humor galore, it's a joyous sight!

www.ingramcontent.com/pod-product-compliance
Lightning Source LLC
Chambersburg PA
CBHW071814160426
43209CB00003B/89